Hug a Bull

An Ode to Animal Dads

Aaron Zenz

WALKER BOOKS FOR YOUNG READERS
AN IMPRINT OF BLOOMSBURY
NEW YORK   LONDON   NEW DELHI   SYDNEY

For *my* dad,
the huggable **Dave Zenz**

Copyright © 2013 by Aaron Zenz

First published in the United States of America in April 2013
by Walker Books for Young Readers, an imprint of Bloomsbury Publishing, Inc.
www.bloomsburykids.com

For information about permission to reproduce selections from this book, write to
Permissions, Walker BFYR, 175 Fifth Avenue, New York, New York 10010

Library of Congress Cataloging-in-Publication Data
Zenz, Aaron.
Hug a bull : an ode to animal dads / by Aaron Zenz.
p.   cm.
Summary: From baby geese to kangaroos to humans, every mom and dad is known by his or her own
special name. Bouncing texts full of fun wordplay and adorable illustrations feature animal parents of every
shape and size, and encourage little readers to express big love. Go ahead and hug a bull!
ISBN 978-0-8027-2824-1 (hardcover) • ISBN 978-0-8027-2825-8 (reinforced)
[1. Stories in rhyme. 2. Animals—Nomenclature—Fiction.] I. Title.
PZ8.3.Z42Hug 2013   [E]—dc23   2012020729

Art created with 42 Prismacolor colored pencils (and 86 broken pencil tips)
Typeset in Arbitrary Regular and Shag Expert Exotica
Book design by Nicole Gastonguay

Printed in China by C&C Offset Printing Co., Ltd., Shenzhen, Guangdong
2   4   6   8   10   9   7   5   3   1   (hardcover)
2   4   6   8   10   9   7   5   3   1   (reinforced)

Take a look—my dad's a **GANDER**.

Take a nap—

our dads are **BOARS.**

Brace yourself—
my dad might **RAM** you.

Our dads might just
DRONE on more.

Father is a dashing **STALLION**.

Father is a
STAG so dear.

Father is a bouncing **BOOMER**.

When Father's home, the **BUCK** stops here.

DRAKE
is what they
call my papa.

TIERCEL
is the name of mine.

Papa is
a wobbly
GOBBLER.

Papa **ROOSTER**, rise and shine!

Do you go riding
with your daddy,

seated on a **SILVERBACK**?

What name does
your daddy go by?

BILLY,

TOM, or maybe

JACK?

My pop's a **HOB**.

My pop's a **COB**.

My pop's a **TOD**, and he's all right.

So love a **BULL** . . .

Adore a **BULL** . . .

Go hug a **BULL**
with all your might.

ALLIGATOR
BULL

ANT
DRONE

BEAR
BOAR

BEE
DRONE

CAT
TOM

CHICKEN
ROOSTER

COW
BULL

DEER
STAG

DONKEY
JACK

DUCK
DRAKE

ELEPHANT
BULL

FERRET
HOB

FOX
TOD

GIRAFFE
BULL

GOAT
BILLY

GOOSE
GANDER

GORILLA
SILVERBACK

HAWK
TIERCEL

HORSE
STALLION

KANGAROO
BOOMER

MOOSE
BULL

MOUSE
BUCK

PIG
BOAR

SHEEP
RAM

SWAN
COB

TURKEY
GOBBLER

WALRUS
BULL

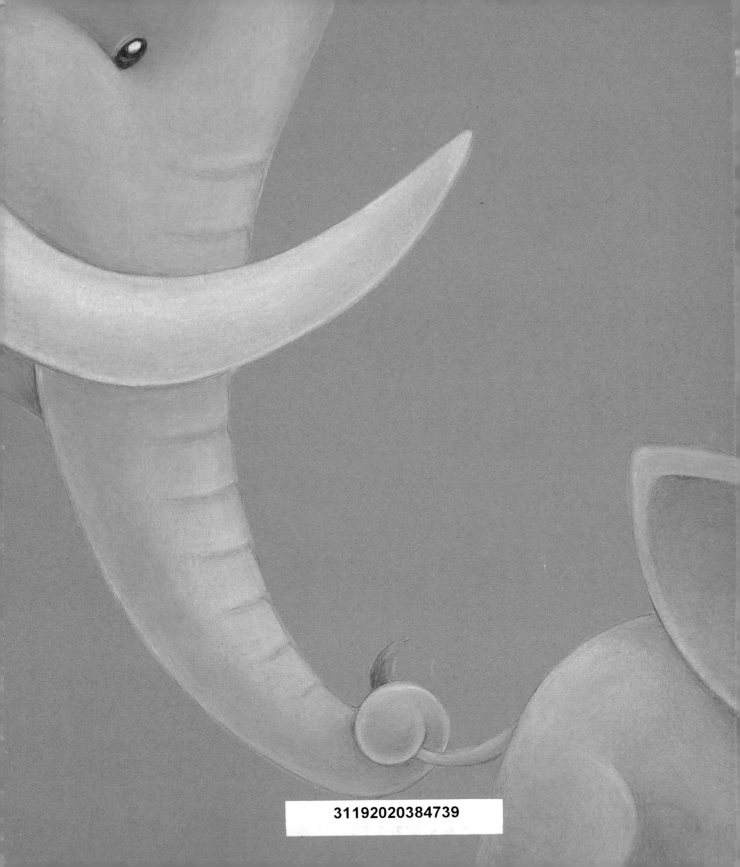